MW01135858

The Step-By-Step Guide to Writing a Novel for Fiction writers and Novelist

By George Lucas

Table of Contents

Introduction

Everybody has a story to tell, a book to write, an epic to create.

If you ask, most people would love to have their own novel created and published. The only problem is that only a very few people have the skill-set required to accomplish this daunting task.

Apart from the obvious lack of skills, the mental barrier is the other most significant hurdle in finishing your own novel. But most professionals and analysts believe that the mental barrier is also only because you lack the particular skills necessary to write a novel. And once you acquire those skills and the knowledge to complete your own book, there will be nothing to stop you.

This book, *"The Step-by-Step Guide to Writing a Novel for Fiction Writers and Novelist"* is written for this exact purpose, i.e., to teach you all the skills and technicalities of writing a novel and to impart the knowledge that most beginners struggle with.

From brainstorming ideas to character development, and from selecting style to editing your own novel, you will learn about each and every aspect of novel writing. Moreover, it is not only the different chapters that will intrigue you. Instead, it is the content — the examples, analogies and the practical tips and tricks — that will benefit you the most.

By the end of this book, you will learn all the important skills, techniques, methods, tips and tricks, that are needed to write the very 1st novel.

This book is divided into 6 major steps — as you can see in the outline of the book. Make sure you go through each and every chapter, so you can fully understand the entire process of writing a novel. Some of the things may seem obvious to you, but do not skip them. There is a lot to learn.

Furthermore, take the content of this book as an inspiration. Read a chapter, brainstorm and find new ideas how you can use this particular information to make your novel better. In other words, do not be limited to the contents of this book. This book is written for the purpose of opening your eyes and expanding your current vision about novel writing, while teaching you all the popular techniques that go into the process.

So let's get started with the 1st chapter of this book.

Chapter 1:
BRAINSTORMING AND
SELECTING IDEAS

Before you start writing the novel, you will need a very solid idea.

And to get that *one solid idea*, you are going to need *"lots of different ideas"*.

You see, most beginners make this crucial mistake of not brainstorming enough ideas. They think that their idea is already the best they could ever come up with. Sometimes, it works. However, more often than not, they later realize that they could have done better.

The topic — or idea — of your novel isn't just about your vision. For it to be a commercial success, there are many factors that you will have to consider before you finalize on a single idea that will take your book further.

In this chapter, we are going to discuss a lot about it.

You will learn how to brainstorm different ideas, determine and understand your target audience, identify potential and profitable ideas that you also have the necessary command in, and select ideas in accordance with the purpose of your book and vision.

Let's get on with it.

Brainstorming Different Ideas

In order to have a bulk of different ideas to select from, you will first have to brainstorm different ideas.

Fortunately, the good part about brainstorming or getting ideas is that they can come to you out of thin air. Ideas come from a whole lot of different places. You can come up with an idea from your life's past experiences. Similarly, you can come up with an idea of how the future — either for you or in general — is going to be. You can think of the lives, struggles, happiness, and difficulties of the people you live with: friends, families, foes, and loved ones. You can easily come up with a lot of good ideas — or a chunk of small ideas — from that one single brainstorming session.

But understand this. In order to come up with several ideas, you will have to understand that brainstorming once is never a good option. You can't sit for 15 minutes, brainstorm, and come up with a heap of different ideas to work from. It does not work this way. As a matter of fact, good ideas hit you when you least expect them. It is actually a gradual process of accumulating several little ideas, often collaging them into something big, and then come up with an extraordinary story that most people would love to hear about.

Last, but not the least, there is one more concept to learn about getting ideas before we move on to discussing the actual techniques.

As most professional writers and novelists believe, ideas may come from several — often unexpected — places. But they rarely come by staring at a blank page. It is a common mistake that many newbie writers so often make. Staring at a blank page in search of a wonderful idea will only get you to a blank page. Nothing more.

But if you know the right techniques, you can turn that blank paper into something special. However, in order for that to happen, you will have to put something on it.

How do you fill a blank paper when you are searching for ideas? Here are a few proven techniques:

1. Free Writing

It is arguably one of the most amazing techniques for fiction writers and novelists. Free writing is also commonly known as "speedwriting" and "free-associating".

Basically, it means non-stop talking to your page. Once you put a lock to your brain and start writing without thinking, your unconscious mind gets a go on the page, and it starts putting wonderful things on the paper.

During free writing, make sure you are not thinking about anything whatsoever. This also means that one second you will write about something, and the next second you will be talking about an entirely different topic. Do not fight it and let it happen. This is the very essence of free writing and it is a proven technique to come up with genuine, new ideas.

2. Making a List

For people who are not comfortable with free writing, making a list is another great option to think of new ideas.

When making a list, make sure you are not writing anything in detail. You just cut off your bullet points into smaller sentences — preferably, words. It keeps your mind fresh for thinking new ideas.

3. A Cluster Diagram

Sometimes, making a list doesn't work either. Some people actually work best in a *visual* environment.

If that is you, the option of creating a cluster diagram is probably your best bet. It will be more user-friendly, visual, and offers the luxury of building on your pre-existing ideas in a more interactive manner.

Coming Up With Ideas

Use the above-mentioned techniques to come up with a whole lot of different ideas. As mentioned earlier, it may take more than one brainstorming session. It's quite fine. Actually, it is preferable.

Spend a few different sessions and come up with several ideas. Once you have a repository of different ideas with either thinking, free writing, making lists or creating a cluster diagram, note them down in a different file.

Do not discard any idea at this stage because you never know which idea turns out to be your biggest success. Moreover, sometimes, smaller or lesser-quality ideas turn out to be a major segment of a different idea in an entirely different story. So, for now, save all your ideas before you move on to our segment, where will be discarding those ideas to identify the one topic to move forward with.

Selecting Ideas

Once you have come up with a few different ideas, it is time to get into the selection process.

There are various factors that go into the process of shortlisting ideas. Here are a few of them:

• Understanding Your Target Audience

First of all, it is important that you have properly identified your target audience. It is the group of people that you are basically writing your novel for.

For example, if your intended target audience are college teenagers, you might want to select an idea that caters to that particular group, e.g., a rom-com college story.

• Understanding the Purpose of Your Book

Similarly, the purpose of your book is also an important factor that goes into the process of selecting a particular idea.

Ask yourself: what is the purpose of writing your book?

Some topics are more commercially viable than others. So if the purpose of writing your book is profits and commercial success, then it will impact your selection process. On the other hand, if your main purpose is to get critical acclamation, then your selected idea might be a little different.

- **<u>Topics That You Have Proper Command In</u>**

The above two points are worth considering to select a particular idea for your novel. However, don't finalize the idea. Not yet.

Gauging the commercial success and identifying your target audience is good, but you can't make a decision on just these two factors. You must have complete command in the topic you are going to write about.

For instance, if, based on the above-mentioned two factors, you are planning to write an intergalactic novel, but you have absolutely no command or knowledge of science, physics or how to cosmic world works, you won't be able to create an interesting read. Moreover, you will always be at a risk of making a stupid error that will ruin your entire novel and its credibility.

In short, you should consider all three of these factors and select an idea that checks each and every box.

<u>Concluding Step 1</u>: Step 1 requires you to brainstorm a few different ideas and select one of them that perfectly fits the bill. It has to be commercially viable, suitable for your target audience, and you also have sufficient knowledge in that topic.

Chapter 2:
CHARACTER DEVELOPMENT

Once you have finalized a basic idea of the topic of your novel, it is time to get into more complex elements of novel-writing.

Kindly note that step no. 2 and step no. 3 can be replaced with each other. It means that once you finalized a basic idea, you can either start outlining the ideas to come up with a basic plot of the story or you can first design its characters.

This is because it works both ways. Sometimes, a story can create its own major characters. And sometimes, once you finish designing a few characters and give them specific personalities and characteristics, they can behave automatically to come up with their own stories.

It basically depends on your own choice and preference. So it is up to you. If you are not comfortable with creating characters without a basic plot, jump on to the next chapter. Or if you prefer building characters before the plot, continue to read on.

Protagonists and Antagonists

It does not matter how many characters you come up for your novel, there will always be at least one protagonist and one antagonist. It is basically the core of your novel — despite the nature of your story.

A protagonist is the good guy or girl of your novel. More often than not, a protagonist is a common and ordinary person who faces extraordinary circumstances to come up on the winning side. This is what makes him / her likable and *larger than life* — what most people like to see.

Moreover, protagonists are usually specialists. They either fight, inspect, drive, do scientific research, enjoy luxuries, make fun of his / her life, or anything in between. It does not matter what, as long as the protagonist is involved in some sort of a specific thing. This is what defines the protagonist until the plot unfolds and he finds himself in some sort of a mess, correlated with the antagonist.

We will talk more about these complexities in this chapter. The protagonist will definitely need several characteristics that define him beyond his profession or other activities, and we will discuss about that very soon.

But for now, understand that your novel always needs a good, larger than life and absolutely lovable protagonist. However, you can always create an antagonist that is often more loved by the protagonist. It all depends on your vision. Sometimes, the writer does not intend it, but the character turns out to be more impressive and interesting than the protagonist himself.

For instance, do you remember the epic that was Christopher Nolan's The Dark Knight? Heath Ledger played the role of the infamous Joker and it instantly became one of the most lovable and memorable characters. It, in no way, indicates that The Batman character played by Christian Bale was of lesser quality. But it shows the dynamic nature of stories and character development. The ideologies, visions and, most of all, the day-to-day activities of a certain character may make him larger than life and absolutely lovable.

Well, coming back to our main topic, as you needed the protagonist, you are also going to need an antagonist. You can either make him absolutely hateful — which is the safest route for most authors — or you can think out of the box and make a good side of him, too.

As mentioned earlier, you will discuss a lot more about it in this chapter.

For now, let's discuss the very logical Yin-and-Yang rule of character development.

The Yin and Yang Rule

Everybody has his own purpose of doing things. Understand that and respect this fact while you are creating your characters and you will go a very long way!

My recommendation would be to never make someone entirely bad or entirely good. Having various shades of grey is a great technique to make your characters interesting, engaging, and more memorable. Moreover, it also keeps your readers on their toes.

This is because if your protagonist is 100% good, it will be very easy for your readers to predict what he is going to do in an upcoming, building scenario. This takes out all the fun. How are you going to create surprises and twists in your story? You will have to consistently introduce new characters to create that drama and that becomes an extremely tedious and difficult process.

So, what is the ideal solution for this problem? Follow the yin and yang rule.

Let me ask you a question. What do you *really* see when you see the very popular icon of the yin and yang image? You know, the black and white swirl?

You see the white image and there is a hint of a black dot in it. On the other hand, you also notice that there is a white section in the black image.

What does it tell you?

It tells you the unpredictability and shades of grey of the human nature. It means that no human being is 100% evil and no human being is 100% good. Everybody has their own little dirty secrets and characteristics that make him / her bad. And these characteristics surface out, if the appropriate situation pops up in the story.

This is what makes characters interesting, engaging and unpredictable. This is what keeps the readers hooked till the end of your book, because they are not 100% sure what might happen.

An Example of Yin-and-Yang Rule

Let me give you an example from the famous book by George R.R. Martin, A Song of Ice and Fire. You might know of this from the popular TV-series franchise, A Game of Thrones.

If you know one of its characters, Jaime Lannister, you will be able to understand what I'm trying to tell you here.

Jaime Lannister was a kings-guard, sworn to protect his king. But one day, he ends up killing the very king he swore to protect. He stabs him in the back when the King least expected it. From thereon, Jaime Lannister was known as The King-slayer — a great insult for a person who took the vow of being a kings-guard for the rest of his life.

For a very long period of time in the story, he never showed any remorse for what did. He was careless, arrogant, and never paid any attention to anyone who called him the King-slayer. He was an out-an-out antagonist in this scenario.

After a couple of books, however, in a moment of vulnerability, he revealed why he killed the king he swore to protect. And once the readers got to know the real reasons behind it, there was a lot of sympathy for Jaime Lannister.

In other words, there was a hint of "white" in an overall "dark" figure. It should be. And it is one of the biggest tips you can learn in character development.

Characterization

By now, you must be toying with a lot of different ideas. The above-mentioned tips and examples would have given your brain plenty to think about. But do not finalize anything yet. There is a lot more you should learn to develop your characters effectively.

In this chapter, we will discuss the various things your characters should have. From their characteristics to their names, we will make your *'characters'* as real as they possibly can be.

The Three-Dimensional Characters

You see, characters are really important. As a matter of fact, a good character always has a past, a present and a future. Think of your characters in such a timeline and it will make a lot of the things easier for you. Moreover, you do not always have to tell your readers everything. You do not always have to tell your readers about the past or future of your characters. That can be implied, but it at least has to be there. Based on the characteristics and qualities of your characters, your readers should be able to imagine their past or the future on their own.

Another great way to add lots of variety in your characters — as well as in your storyline — is by assigning each character his or her own little secret.

It adds a lot of depth and richness in the content of your book and the personality of your characters.

Note that the secret may or may not have to directly relate to the main story. It might not even have anything to do with the content of your book. But by just keeping it there — in a repository — you unlock numerous potential areas that you could not have explored otherwise.

Those secrets can also become the *motivation* to connect the characters with your main story. And this brings us to our next point ...

Motivation to Connect With Your Story

Once you define the past, present and future of your characters, it makes it easier for you to connect them with your main story.

Simply speaking, based on their characteristics, those characters should have an inherent motivation to be connected with the main story of your novel. It may be a past experience or a future vision that becomes the reason why they are going to connect to your main story. But it has to be something.

Making your characters jump into your story without any solid reason makes it seem odd and out of the blue.

Passions, Desires, Opinions and Feelings

It can easily be termed as one of the most important aspects of character development. Once you master this process of characterization, the process of character development will become a lot simpler and easier to you.

First of all, focus on giving each of your characters a unique personality and a set of traits. These traits define each of your characters and the actions they take later on. If you assign each character a very distinct personality with as many traits as possible, it helps you a lot when it comes to story development. This is because most of the time, when you are stuck at some stage of your story or plot-twist, you can ask yourself what a certain character would do in such a position. Based on that answer, you can move forward. It is a great practice.

Make sure each character in your novel has passions, desires, opinions and feelings of his / her own. The character should be able to decide on its own, anticipate, outsmart other characters, respond to difficult situations in a unique way, and come up with solutions that even the readers can somewhat expect because of his given personality.

At this stage, you should be wondering that if you give so much away about your book's characters and define their characteristics so vividly, wouldn't it become very boring for the readers? After all, we do not want them to become completely predictable as it takes out all the fun and makes your book boring and uninteresting. But this is very different to the scenario we discussed earlier.

You see, describing the traits and personality of a characters helps you understand the way a certain character behaves. But it does not absolutely define them. And this is the exact reason why I first recommended to use the Yin-and-Yang rule, as it always keeps a few surprises for the readers.

Given said that, a little predictability is good — and often necessary for a successful novel. This is because readers want to connect with your characters. They want to be emotionally attached to them. More importantly, they often want to live the situation your characters lived in the book. In order to make this fantasy of your readers true, your characters will have to be a little predictable so the readers can safely say, *"Yes, I know that character"*.

Always remember that there is a fine line between being unpredictable and giving it all away. You will have to keep the right balance in order to bring life to your characters as well as to your book and overall story.

Names of Your Characters

When you are developing your characters, make sure to give them appropriate names.

Unfortunately, most beginners do not pay enough attention to this important aspect of character development. They just assign random names to random characters and it goes a long way destroying the credibility of their imagined characters. Furthermore, many authors also just give some of their favorite names to random characters and be done with it. This approach cannot be any more wrong.

There are a lot of things that go into naming a particular character. Some of the factors that you will have to consider are:

- The age of that particular character

- His or her role in the story

- Various traits of that character. For instance, if you are naming a ruthless, muscular spy, you should not name him "Bob". It does not go with that personality and image. Instead, a name like "Jason Roy" would suit him better.

Furthermore, another important tip to remember is that do not name multiple characters with similar pronunciations. It is absolutely important to remember your primary goal: to tell your story as clearly as possible. If you assign two different characters somewhat similar names, it will only confuse your readers.

Apart from that, never use famous celebrity names. Instead, choose less obvious names to make your characters stand out. This is important because when you name one of your characters for a celebrity name, it comes with a baggage. Your readers already have a certain image of that celebrity in their heads, and if your character is in anyway different from that celebrity in real life, your readers will find it difficult to make the transition.

Here are a few more tips to name some of your characters:

- If you want to name tough guys, think of hard consonants, e.g., R or G.

- If you want to name beautiful girls and women, soft vowels or consonant sounds are always a better option,e.g., S, M, O, Y.

Secondary Characters

Secondary characters are and should always be less important than your main characters — protagonists and antagonists.

I would hardly recommend not to include too many secondary characters in your book, as it can often unnecessarily complicate things. However, if your story demands it, by all means go for it.

Sometimes, you even realize that two of your secondary characters can be combined into one single character. This, although limits the dynamism of the story, can really simplify things for your readers.

However, you may need to create a *foil*.

If you do not know, a *foil* is the protagonist's companion. The best part about the foil is that it is often completely different to your main character in terms of personality, traits, wit, interests, stature or even age. One of the best examples that I can remember at the moment is of Dr. Watson in Sherlock Holmes.

You can easily see the massive differences between the character of Sherlock Holmes and Dr. Watson. Both of them are absolutely different to each other in almost every aspect, yet the foil always accompanies the protagonist.

The primary importance of foil is that it emphasizes the characteristics of the protagonist. Because of the contrasting nature, you can easily see and identify some of the "hidden" characteristics and personality traits of your main character. Moreover, when both the protagonist and the foil are posed by a difficult situation, they often choose the solve it in completely different fashions. This can help you with the storyline by paving way to a conflict, twist, or just plain old dynamism.

Creating Profiles of Your Characters

Once you have done the handwork of naming your characters, adding personality traits, secrets, and other important characteristics, note it down altogether.

In other words, create index cards for each of your characters. Create their profiles, so they can be memorable. Moreover, it will also help you to weed out any errors or bloopers in your characterization process.

You can go and add as many things as you would like to add in this character profile. The richer the content, the better it is.

But if you are not too sure of what to include in it, here are a few things you must include in your characters' profiles:

1. The name of the character

2. Any nickname that you are going to use in your novel

3. The age of the character

4. His or her entire family tree — whether or not those family members are in the story or not.

5. Personality traits and characteristics of your character.

6. One word that could easily define the character in his entirety.

7. The secrets — hidden or revealed — of that character.

8. His primary motivation

9. The name of all the people that character loves and really cares for

10. The name of all those people that the character hates ... and also the reasons why

11. Write three adjectives that can efficiently define that particular character

12. A few words about your character's physical appearance.

13. Your character's strength

14. Your characters' fears

15. His or her talking style

Another tip is to visualize your characters as much as you can. When defining physical features, find an image of the person your characters resembles the most. If you can, sketch. It gives your characters a lot of depth.

For instance, do you remember when the first book of the Harry Potter series was released? There was a very distinct image of Mr. Harry Potter — his hairstyle, his round-shaped glasses, and the infamous mark on his forehead. That same image was then emulated in the movies, and every single viewer was able to connect with that description they first read in the book.

This should be your approach, too.

Concluding Step 2: _Step 2 requires you to develop all the characters of your book._

Think of all the characters you are going to need for your selected idea, and start creating separate profiles for each of them. Make sure to add lots of information in each profile.

Chapter 3:
Outlining the Ideas

Let's see where we are.

By now, you should have brainstormed several different ideas. Out of that reservoir, you must have shortlisted a few good ideas and decided on one of them that will be the main topic of your novel.

Moreover, you must have also designed your characters. You now know the differences between the protagonist, antagonist, foil, and other secondary characters. Furthermore, we have already discussed in detail the various aspects of characterization, adding personality and traits, naming the characters, and creating their images in either your head or on a piece of paper.

If you have done everything right by now, you are in a great position to get started with the main story of your novel. And this is going to be the third step in this wonderful journey of creating your own book.

In this chapter, we will discuss how to outline the ideas of your main story. You will also learn the very popular bun-analogy that will simplify your story-telling process. In short, you will learn a lot about how to move forward with your novel.

Having an Outline

Having an outline can be somewhat debatable. But it is definitely one of the best ways to get started with your story, without having to worry about the effectiveness of your sentences.

Understand "an outline" as the game of jigsaw puzzle. Do you remember that?

When playing the jigsaw puzzle game, you spread out all the pieces in a complete mess. When you throw them out on the table, you can see of all the pieces at once. Then you start rearranging them in their correct intended order.

Outlining your ideas and storyline is great. It helps you organize your thoughts, especially when you are just starting with a new story.

You see, with a new story, you are not 100% sure how it is going to move forward. A good story has a powerful beginning, a captivating middle, and a very memorable end. Besides all that, you will have to introduce several characters in between that. Some of those characters will have to be introduced in the beginning of the story, while some of them will be introduced later. The introduction of those characters also leads to new situations — or conflicts. With so many things happening all at once, you can easily get confused. This is why outlining your ideas before you start writing your first draft is a great practice.

As you are now fully aware of the various benefits of having a well-structured and organized outline, let's discuss the various techniques that can help you in this process.

Creating Themes

Before you start outlining the main story of your book, you will first need to have a proper theme for it.

The best and most recommended way to find a theme is to think one out of thin air. A good novelist follows his heart and is not afraid to take a few risks. Besides, if you have already carefully chosen your target audience and the main story of your book, you have minimized the risk. So you can afford a little bit of creativity and personal vision here.

The key is to follow your ideas rather than forcing them in a certain direction. If you have a knack of generating good ideas, you will do particularly good in this segment.

When you think of multiple themes, you will find a lot of useless ideas that you can't put in your story. However, at the same time, you will also find a few good ideas that can be turned into proper sequences. Some of the ideas might also be used as the background experiences of certain characters. When you combine all those ideas in proper sequences, a very solid theme will emerge out of it. You can then start writing on that particular theme to start filling up the pages of your book.

Sounds simple enough, right?

Let me give you a very interesting example.

I will again talk about George R.R. Martin here. A Song of Ice and Fire is an extremely popular book and its TV adaptation, A Game of Thrones is one of the most popular TV shows ever. It's a very complicated and multi-dimensional story, but very few people know how George came up with its idea.

There is a rather minor scene in the first book that shows a young boy who finds 5 baby dire-wolves in a forest.

The idea struck George and he instantly realized that this idea had so much more potential than that. He noted it down and came up with a few more ideas — in that setting — to make one heck of an overall theme.

In short, by thinking of multiple ideas, following them instead of forcing them, and combining them in a logical sequence, you can come up with a very solid theme for your novel.

Using Index Cards

Finding different ideas for a theme is easy; arranging them in proper sequences is a bit difficult. The best way of doing that is by using index cards.

Using index cards allows you to arrange your ideas into patterns and sequence them in their most logical orders. Moreover, index cards make it extremely easy to move ideas around. And having each idea — or sequence — on a piece of paper helps you see different connections between them.

And do you know the best part about using index cards? It is very common to make mistakes when you are creating an outline for your idea, but if you are using index cards, it becomes very easy to move them and make a new outline or sequence.

On the other hand, if you directly start writing the content of your book without first having a well-structured and organized outline, you will have to write and rewrite the entire content multiple times if you commit any mistake.

There is one important thing to note before you can start creating an outline. It is to understand that each story has three parts: a beginning, a middle, and an end. When you are arranging your ideas into proper sequences, make sure to find patterns in your ideas. Moreover, in a bird's eye view, you should be able to see a definite pattern in your theme, that is has a beginning, a middle, and an end.

The Bun-Analogy

Although the concept is very simple to understand, but the bun-analogy (as most novelists like to call it) makes it fun and memorable.

Imagine a bun. How does it look like?

First of all, it has a top bun. Then the filling comes in the middle, and it has pretty much everything in it. Then comes the bottom bun that has been holding it all together till now.

The story of your novel should be exactly like this.

The beginning of your story is like the top bun. It gives the readers something to bite on, introduce them to what is to come next, and gives a proper idea of how your story is going to be.

Then comes the middle part, where the story throws all kinds of stuff at you. It introduces different characters. Moreover, it is the middle part of the story where plot-twists and conflicts emerge. As the middle part of the bun has everything in it, the middle stage of your story gives the readers all kinds of different stuff — new characters, twists, conflicts, etc.

Last, but not the least, there comes the bottom bun. It is what that has been holding the entire thing together till now. It is the conclusion that most people wait for. Moreover, it is the bottom bun — the end of the story — that holds a few surprises down the road. You may find a few things there that you never thought the bun (or the story) even had. And if you want your readers to end the story completely satisfied, the last part of your novel — just like the bottom bun — has to be very interesting and satisfactory.

Storyboarding

Storyboarding is another important step before writing the first draft. Generally speaking, it can either supplement the above-mentioned processes of outlining your ideas and combining them into one theme, or it can altogether replace that entire process. It eventually depends on your own personal choice and preference.

Let's briefly explain what storyboarding is, so you can then decide how to use it for your own novel.

Storyboarding is basically a visual display of all your major story elements, characters, twists, and notions. These elements can be then moved around the timeline to better serve the purpose of the story. Moreover, different situations that arise within the story either after a twist or by the introduction of new characters, will also have a role to play in it.

Moving these elements in a timeline can help you visualize things in a linear fashion. Apart from that, it also helps you organize and imagine situations and their relationships with certain characters, sequence and twists of the story.

Lastly, there is one more thing you can do in this regard. In fact, I would recommend doing it anyway — whether you are storyboarding or not.

Create a straight line across a piece of paper and make it a timeline of your story. On that timeline, you can then add page numbers or word-count to see your story in a much better fashion.

For example, if you believe you would need 100,000 words to make a worthy novel in your genre, write 0 on the left side of the timeline, and write 100,000 on the right side of it.

Once you have done it, mark where you will introduce different characters on the timeline. You should also include major plot changes, twists, and conflicts on the timeline — where you think they should appear.

Do not worry if you do not get it perfectly right in the first attempt. You will never get it right. The key here is to put ideas on a piece of paper before you start writing the content of the book. You will have a general idea of how and when things will happen in your main story.

For instance, if you have marked the introduction of the antagonist at 25% on the timeline, you will have a general idea how you need to build-up to that and when you should be introducing the antagonist.

***Concluding Step 3**: Outline your ideas is very important. This step requires you to create index cards that will later help you arrange and rearrange the important events of your story.*

Chapter 4:
SELECTING STYLES

By now, you must have selected a solid idea for the story of your novel, designed characters, and outlined the theme.

Now it is time to finalize the styles you are going to use throughout your book.

It is another very important aspect that most beginners just do not pay any attention to. However, after the basic plot and power of characters, it is your writing that is going to leave the biggest impression on your readers. If the styles that you use in the novel aren't matching a certain standard, your writing will look dull, unimaginative and boring. You do not want that.

This is why selecting styles prior to writing the book is extremely important. In this chapter, you are going to learn several important rules of selecting styles. Moreover, you will also learn the major differences between the two popular narration styles — the 1st person narration style and the 3rd person narration style.

So let's get started.

Selecting a Narration Style

Selecting a narration style is probably going to be the biggest decision you will make in this section of the book.

It is the narration style that can fuel a lot of energy into the book, and you have to choose it in accordance with the context and story of your novel.

Let me first briefly explain the two major types of narration styles. After that, we will discuss the pros and cons of each other.

The 1st Person Narration Style

The 1st person narration style is definitely a popular one, and more and more modern authors are adopting this style.

It is the type of narration style in which you get into the main character's shoes and sees the world in the novel as that character does. Because of this, the 1st person narration style is definitely more personal and engaging.

Given said that, it also has a few disadvantages.

First of all, the 1st person narration style will limit you as a writer. Since you are telling the story from a character's POV, you cannot explain your readers what is going on in the scenes where the main character isn't present. This makes the process of storytelling a bit difficult and confined. Another drawback is that the 1st person narration style requires the narrating character's interference most of the times. This can be frustrating for the readers as well as the writer of the book.

However, at the same time, the advantages of the 1st person narration style is that it is personal and seems more capable in engaging readers. Moreover, it gives the exact view to the readers, which may make the reading experience more pleasant and real. Lastly, most creative writers prefer writing it this way, as it often comes more naturally to them.

Some of the modern examples of the 1st person narration style include:

1. The Twilight Saga

2. The Hunger Games

3rd Person Narration Style

Unlike the 1st person narration style, the 3rd person narration style offers a lot more freedom to the writers. However, it may not create the same level of interest as the 1st person narration style, especially if your writing is not that good.

But do not take it the wrong way. There have been some great, epic novels written in the 3rd person narration style. A few very popular examples are:

1. The Harry Potter Series

2. The Lord of the Rings

Those books did great! Your book can perform with the 3rd person narration style, too. In fact, more serious readers actually prefer the 3rd person narration style over the more amateur 1st person narration style.

The biggest disadvantage — relatively speaking — of the 3rd person narration style is that it doesn't seem that personal as the 1st person narration style. Secondly, it does not give the same experience as the 1st person narration style.

Given said that, the 3rd person narration style also has a few distinct advantages. First of all, it is the most ideal route to describe a slightly complex and multi-dimensional story. Since the narrating character does not have to be present all the time in all the different times and places, the 3rd person narration style allows you the luxury to explain the readers what is going on in the background.

Moreover, unlike the 1st person narration style, the 3rd person narration style does not have to follow the same voice and style of the narrating character. It is more like a narration by the writer himself and, therefore, you can use whichever voice you feel most comfortable with. Otherwise, in the 1st person narration, you often have to carry the same voice and style as that of the narrating character — which is often the main character of the story.

Which Narration Style Should You Choose?

You have now learned the pros and cons of both the narration styles. The ultimate choice depends upon the option *you* are most comfortable with. But make sure to take your audience in the account, too. This is because if your target audience does not particularly like the 1st person narration style, but you do it anyway just because you feel comfortable with that, your novel may not get great reviews. It is important to consider each and every aspect before you decide on a particular writing style.

If you are not too sure about the preferences of your target audience, you can always conduct a small survey. Target a few people and specifically ask them which narration style they usually prefer.

Moreover, if you do not have any such resources to survey your target audience, there is another technique. Grab a few popular books in your genre that are released recently. Notice their narration style. And if you are equally comfortable in both the 1st person and the 3rd person narration style, choose the one that is popular across all those books. Just make sure you only research the recently popular books within your genre.

Syntax

Simply speaking, syntax refers to the way you put your words together and create a sentence.

Being a writer, you can make really simple sentences, with the most common sentence structure, which is,

Subject + Verb + Object.

But it does not always have to be this way. As a professional writer, it is your job to make your writing interesting and engaging to the readers, but without making it too complicated to understand.

Sometimes, a very simple sentence would do the job. However, sometimes, you often need to explain and elaborate things further to help the readers understand what you are trying to tell them. In such scenarios, the syntax will vary, different phrases, adjectives, and clauses will have to be added, and the usual order of the words might also be changed drastically.

Here are a few examples.

i. My office is full of insects, which I hate so much.

ii. Insects! I hate them.

iii. Insects! I have lots of insects in my office and I hate them all.

iv. I hate insects, but my office is full of them.

v. My office is full insects and I hate them. But I don't hate ants. They are rather cute. I like them.

Notice each of the examples are different, and they all convey different meanings with relatively similar words and concepts.

When you are writing a novel, it is important to identify which type of syntax are you going to use. Moreover, you can even assign different sentence structures to different characters to make your novel seem more exciting, engaging and dynamic.

But do note that it will make things quite difficult for you, the writer.

Voice

Just like the structure of your sentences, "voice" also has a lot to do in your novel.

Having a good voice will help you keep your readers sane and engaged in your story. And if you don't do it right, it can easily backfire and ruin the entire experience.

If you choose the 1st person narration style, you will have to emulate the voice of your narrating character. For instance, in the popular Twilight series, the narrating character was the lead heroine, Bella Swan. She was a rather timid and confused girl and it reflected in the writing. But the same cannot be said for the Harry Potter books, as there is no 1st person narration style. The voice is completely different in both the series.

So choose your particular voice wisely. It should be one in which your target audience and you are totally comfortable. If you are using the 1st person narration style, just create an in-depth and comprehensive character profile for your narrating character, come up with the natural voice of that character, and try to emulate it as closely you possible can. This will be your best bet.

One more thing before we end this discussion on the topic of "voice". There are two types of sentences that writers generally use: active voice and passive voice.

Generally speaking, passive voice sentences are vague and confusing, and you should avoid them as much as you can. Replace the passive voice sentences with the active voice sentences whenever possible. They are simple and easy to understand.

Choice of Words

One of the most beautiful things of the English language is that there are plenty of synonyms for each and every word. This gives you a lot of options to choose from.

However, it can easily be very frustrating for the writer to decide which word should be used in a particular scenario, or in the general voice of the story.

Each such word may mean exactly the same, but they should be used in different manners to serve different purposes.

Here are a few examples that will help clear the picture:

i. The average house contains <u>quite a few</u> roaches.

ii. The average house contains <u>heaps of</u> roaches.

iii. The average house contains <u>numerous</u> roaches.

iv. The average house contains <u>tons of</u> roaches.

v. The average house contains <u>hundreds of</u> roaches.

As you can see, selecting different words may send a completely different message to your readers. In the first example, the message is that there a few roaches, but it does not send any sort of a dangerous signal. The readers will be able to easily forget it. However, in the second example, the message is that there are an alarming number of roaches that the house-owners should be worried about.

So when choosing words for the content of your book, you will have to be very careful. First, determine what kind of message are you trying to send with that particular sentence or group of words. Once you have fully determined the type of message you want to send and the kind of impact it is going to have on the story of your novel, use the most appropriate word for it. You will often have to read between the lines to find out the message it is going to convey to your readers.

Contractions

You can either use contractions or full words in your novel. It is not a very big thing but it can set the overall mood of your story.

One rule that you should be aware of is to never use contractions in formal writing. So if the tone of your novel is extremely formal, you are better without using the contractions.

On the other hand, if one of your characters talk in a very formal fashion, it is important not to use contractions in his or her dialogue. All such small things increase the credibility of your writing.

Selecting Styles Based on Different Characters

In this chapter, you learned all there is about identifying and choose styles for your novel. But you do not always have to keep up with only 1 particular style.

There is another option. You can select different styles based on different characters. With this option, you can customize different voices, syntax, writing styles, use of contractions, use of formal and informal styles, different choices of words: all based on different characters.

But be aware. While it does seem tempting and takes your novel on a whole new level of dynamism and variety, it can open a pandora box that can be very difficult to handle for most beginners. So choose it wisely, and only if you feel 100% confident in handling all those different styles for different characters.

<u>Concluding Step 4</u>: In step 4, you should identify particular writing styles and keep it uniform throughout the novel. Moreover, also determine whether you are going to use the 1st person narration style or the 3rd person narration style. Only after that, you should jump on to the next chapter.

Chapter 5:
Writing Your First Draft

Congratulations! By now, you have done pretty much everything a novelist should do before writing the first draft.

You have selected an idea for your story; you have your characters fully developed; you have outlined the ideas and theme of your novel; and you have determined the particular narration style you would use in your novel. Excellent!

After all that tedious and hard work, it is time to get yourself a reward. It is time to start creating the first draft of your novel.

And while it does seem really simple to start writing, there is a lot of science that goes into the writing process. In this chapter, we are going to discuss some of the important rules and tips and tricks to writing your first draft.

Showing, Not Telling

Do you know the essence of writing a book? It is to help your readers visualize what you are trying to tell them.

This is the very reason why most creative persons would rather enjoy a good book than a great movie. Movies ruin imaginations. Films do not allow the viewers to imagine anything else than what they are seeing on their screens. However, books are not that limiting at all. They actually create the perfect setting to encourage more imagination and visualization.

This is why you need to make your writing more interesting, engaging and appealing. So the idea is to **show, not tell** your readers what the scene is about, how your character looks and behave in certain situations, how the world of your novel looks like, and everything in between.

Another important tip for when you are writing your first draft is to be very, very specific. Imaginative writing — like that you so often find in novels — is all about specificity and particular events. A novel can be a good reflection of a writer's inner self. And no novel can ever be great if the writer keeps using abstract or vague language. So make sure you always describe events in specificity. When you are writing about items from your outline, make them particular incidents, instead of vague thoughts. Describe how a particular event takes place to a certain character, on what date or time of the day, and **how** — not what — the characters respond to that. It's the art of storytelling.

If the readers can "see" how a certain event is happening in the story of your novel, it will a lot more interesting to them. It is important that your readers feel the emotions going through in your story. In order to this, you will have to be a little more wordy and descriptive. But do not pay a lot of attention to it, as you will weed out the unnecessary words and other such issues during the editing phase.

Here is an example of two different types of sentences. One is a vague sentence, while other is very descriptive. Read the following sentences and guess which sentence gave you more information about the particular event happening, and which scene were you better able to visualize and imagine.

i. She felt nervous.

ii. Her legs tensed up, her stomach felt fluttery, and her hands were suddenly cold and clammy.

Didn't the second example was more specific and easy to imagine? Your writing should be like this.

The Power Of 'GOS' and 'GFS'

Writing your first draft is all about starting with the flow and keeping up with it throughout the course. We will talk more about it next.

But for now, understand that it is very important to keep going. Unfortunately, there is one major hurdle that prevents most beginners from starting with their first drafts. It is the 'GOS'.

The 'GOS', which is also commonly known as the Great Opening Sentence, is what troubles beginners the most. Do not be stumped by the GOS.

Don't take me wrong, though. The 'GOS' or the Great Opening Sentence is extremely important — perhaps, one of the most important part of your entire novel. This is because it is this opening sentence that draws the readers in and encourages them to keep going line after line, till they reach the very last word of the book. It is that very first impression that makes the rest of the image for someone. It is the reflection of the quality of your novel.

But is it worth waiting for? Will you ever come up with the perfect 'GOS' to start your novel? Or more importantly, do you have to *wait* till you get that perfect combination of words?

The answer is a big NO!

Nothing is worthy enough to stop your writing process. If you have fully accomplished all the tasks that are mentioned in this book till now, you have done everything you needed to do. So do not wait for the perfect 'GOS' or you will waste precious time.

If you are absolutely stuck with the 'GOS', here are a few tips for you:

i.   See if you could start your GOS with 'Once upon a Time'. You can always change it and reword the sentence to a more appropriate version, but it gives you a good head-start in the right direction.

ii. You can start by explaining the setting of a particular scene.

iii. You can also start by introducing a certain character and what that character is doing in that particular scene of your novel. This technique is often used in the 1st person narration style.

iv. The 'GOS' can also be started by simply explaining what the book is about. This technique is especially helpful in the 3rd person narration style.

Although I do not have to explain the concept of 'GFS' at this stage, but since we already discussing the 'GOS', I guess it makes sense to wrap it up now.

The 'GFS' refers to the Great Final Sentence. It is what makes that long-lasting final impression on your readers, which eventually transforms your book from *good* to *great!*

Just like the 'GOS', the 'GFS', too, will take a lot of time and effort. But it is a lot easier to handle than the 'GOS', for two main reasons:

i. It does not stop you from starting with your first draft of the novel.

ii. As the 'GFS' is always at the end of the book, you already have a lot of idea on how to end the story with the perfect 'GFS'.

So the key here is not to worry about the 'GFS' at this stage. Right now, your only focus should be on writing your first draft. Perfecting every sentence would come later — in the editing phase. Moreover, 'GFS' would always be a very long way down the road.

Keeping the Flow

It is tempting to get your story right the very first time, but it is a big ask and one that you should not pursue.

You see, unless you are sitting on a final exam, you have as many opportunities to rewrite as you like. There is no limit, and it is a great luxury to have.

The pressure of doing it right the very first time can be tremendous, and it is the very reason why most writers get stuck before they even start writing their first draft.

Understand this basic concept. First drafts are usually the ones that writers throw away, so do not worry too much about it. Your goal should be to start writing and keeping the flow as much as possible.

I cannot emphasize enough the importance of actually *start writing*. This is what this particular section is all about. There are various tips which you will have to apply at this stage of your novel-writing process — all of which will help you to get over the line.

Here are a few such tips to help you get started with the first draft:

i. Consider first draft for what it is, i.e,. just your first attempt at something. Do not take it too seriously.

ii. Do not think, *'I am now starting my novel'*. This brings undue pressure that only halts your progress. Instead, think, *'Now I am writing my first draft'*. It will take much of the pressure off.

iii. You can also vow not to show this first draft to anybody. Once the fear of social rejection and being criticized is taken off the table, it becomes a lot easier to actually get started without having to worry about perfecting every little detail.

iv. Most beginners find it difficult to get started with their first draft because they are not sure how to take off with their story. The best way to avoid this is to write about whichever scene comes first to you. Since you would already have an outline, you can write whichever scene you want to write about. Once done, you can then write about other scenes of your story and then combine them in accordance with the logical sequence of the novel.

There is nothing much to discuss about writing your first draft. It all depends on the story of your novel, its characters, and the way you want to approach it. The only thing that is worth discussing is how to keep writing and finish your first draft as soon as possible.

Always remember that writing the first draft is the first — and probably the most important — aspect of finishing your novel. Do not worry too much about the accuracy of your story, the actions of your characters, and the unfolding of events at this stage — provided they are in line with the initial theme and plot.

You will iron out all the issues in the editing and revision phase — which is our next point to discuss.

Concluding Step 5: Step 5 requires you to write the first draft of the novel. Do not focus on perfecting it the first time. It's almost impossible to get it right the very first time. Instead, the primary goal of your first draft is to keep you going.

Chapter 6:
REVISION, EDITING AND REWRITING

This is going to be your last step before you can finish your novel.

In the previous chapter, we talked about the importance of getting started without worrying too much about the writing and other technicalities. At that stage, the important thing was to keep going and maintaining the flow.

Now comes the revising, editing and rewriting phase in which you iron out the errors, mistakes and other blunders you made in the first draft.

This chapter can be divided into three different sections, which are:

- Revising

- Editing

- Rewriting

Understanding each of these sections would help you a great deal.

Let's start from the top.

1. Revising

In the world of novel-writing, revising literally means "re-seeing" the contents of your book.

Unlike the contrary belief, 'revising' does not require you to fix grammatical errors or spelling mistakes. Instead, in this phase, you will try to find and fix bigger problems.

For example, structural problems, plot loopholes, etc. When you are revising the contents of your book, look at the bigger picture and try to see the entire shape of your story. Having such a bird's eye view will help you identify major problems with your novel. More importantly, it will help you identify places where you need to add content, subtract content, or move content from one place to another (rearranging).

Try the Two-Step Process

In this phase, when you are trying to get rid of bigger, structural problems, you have to do 2 different things: finding the problems and fixing them.

It will be very tempting to do both of them at the same time, but it is the wrong way and you should avoid it.

First of all, you need to find all the problems that are in your book. Only when you have identified all the problems, you should then start fixing them.

The concept is to find the problems before your reader do. And in order to find such problems, you will have to be in your readers shoes. How can you do that? It is simple. Just start reading your book from cover to cover like a normal reader does.

The idea is to get a feeling of your novel as a whole. You cannot do it if you are stopping every now and then for rectifying errors as you get them. Make sure you have a pen in your hand when you are revising. Whenever you find an error, just mark it and move on. Do not waste your time by stopping to fix things.

Moreover, being a writer, always trust your gut feelings. If you believe there is something wrong in a particular section of your book, chances are it is, and your readers will find it, too.

Another tip is to read your book aloud. By hearing the words, you will have a quite different experience. It will significantly help in the revision process.

2. Editing

Once you are done revising your book, reading it from cover to cover, and fixing out all the structural problems in the end, it is time to get into the editing phase.

Generally speaking, editing means making your novel as reader-friendly and simple as possible. It also means improving the structure of your sentences, rectifying any grammatical errors, and fixing spelling errors.

After the revision phase, the editing phase is the next logical step to go with.

The first rule of editing is to always use 'appropriate' sentence structures and spellings. Remember that in the world of writing, there is no right or wrong. This is why I used the word 'appropriate' — and not 'correct'.

Use the type of sentence structures and spelling that your target audience is most comfortable with. However, do not compromise on the quality of your writing.

The best part about novel-writing is that it offers you a lot of freedom. Unlike essays or business writing, imaginative writing allows you to play fat and loose with accepted rules of English language to achieve a desired outcome or a particular effect. So feel free to play with it during the editing phase and achieve the exact effect you want to achieve with a certain paragraph, sentence or a word.

You will have to read your entire book quite a few times to edit out all the issues in it. In a book over 100,000 words, there will always be a few mistakes that your eyes will skip. So do not be too hesitant in hiring a professional editor to do one last round of editing — when you are done on your own.

Got all the tips?

So let's move on to a few specific questions that you should be asking yourself during this editing phase.

9 Questions to Ask Yourself While Editing Your Novel

Ask yourself the following 9 questions to complete the editing phase.

Q. No.1: Is this the most effective style for this particular piece of novel?

Ask yourself if this is the most appropriate style you could come up with. For instance, if you are working on a comedy novel, the style and voice will be funny, quirky and light-hearted. It will certainly be very different from a serious drama.

Q. No.2: Have I followed that particular style consistently throughout the book?

It is important to select a particular style and follow it throughout the book. If you keep sliding from formal to informal, funny to serious, and slangy to pompous, you will never be able to engage your readers. It will be more like a roller-coaster ride when it should have been more interesting, engaging and credible.

Q. No.3: Is the content of your book simple and easy to understand?

Nobody likes to read confusing sentences. People read books to learn and be entertained. There is no point in reading a book if it does not help them to do either of those things.

So the question to be asked is that the content of your book simple and easy to understand, or is it going to confuse the readers?

Q. No. 4: Do all my subjects agree with their verbs?

It is one of the most common mistakes, so make sure you pay a lot of extra attention to it. You might know this as "subject-verb agreement".

Q. No. 5: Are all of my sentences complete?

You never leave an incomplete sentence. However, when you are writing a novel, you may leave a few incomplete sentences that you definitely shouldn't.

Q. No. 6: Have I properly punctuated the entire book?

Punctuation is important. There is a lot of difference in "Let's eat, grandma" and "Let's eat grandma".

It is absolutely crucial to have your punctuations right throughout the book. A single mistake may lead to a completely different scenario — one that you never intended in the first place, just like the above-mentioned example.

Q. No. 7: Have I used apostrophes in the right places?

Apostrophes often make lives miserable. They are those little misplaced commas that either show possession or are used for making contractions.

It is important to follow a definite style throughout the book. For instance, if you haven't used contractions because you are writing a formal book, make sure you follow the same style everywhere.

Q. No. 8: Have I put paragraph breaks in all the right places?

Generally speaking, paragraph breaks are used to end an idea and start a new one. It is a very basic rule to start every new idea with a different paragraph. But the problem with imaginative writing and novels is that ideas are often intertwined into each other. They are not as specific and clear-cut as they would be in an essay or business writing.

If you find it too confusing to identify where you should put paragraph breaks, follow this simple advice.

As a writer, your instinct is your greatest weapon. You know your story better than anyone else, so use that instinct to put paragraph breaks. Whenever you feel the ideas are turning corners or taking a breath, make a new paragraph.

Furthermore, as a general rule of thumb, do not exceed your sentence to more than 17 words. Similarly, do not have more than 5 such sentences in a single paragraph. If you type on computers and have 8 typed lines in a single paragraph, try to break that text into 2 different paragraphs.

Q. No. 9: Is my spelling correct?

There is not a lot here to talk about. Just make sure that all the spellings in your book is 100% correct. There is nothing worse than having a spelling error in a professional novel.

Apart from that, if your target audience is British, use their spellings. If your target audience is American, use their spelling rules.

3. Rewriting

Here comes the last part this chapter.

Rewriting means adding content, removing content, and rearranging content from one place to another.

When do you need that?

Here are a few possible scenarios when you might need to rewrite your content:

A. You might need to cut content when you come across any of the following things:

i. Too much unnecessary background information that stalls the main story for too long.

ii. Overly long dialogues

iii. Things that are already said in the book

iv. Facts and truths that do not need to be told or the ones that the readers must have already figured out by themselves.

v. Anything after the main ending of the story.

B. You might need to add content here:

- Important facts that you know, but your readers don't.

- When you have only *told* but didn't *show* the readers.

- The kind of important details that make the story come to life.

- A better GOS or GFS.

C. Rearrange the following texts to make your story better:

i. A confusing part of the story that often jumps backwards and forwards in time.

ii. Parts of the story that suddenly jump to explain a different character's POV.

iii. Unnecessary information that interrupts a powerful and pivotal scene.

iv. A surprising fact that basically reveals the ending of the story. It should be moved to the end.

There will be times when you will be tempted not to make the necessary changes. Your brain will trick you in reading the text 2 or 3 times and it will gradually start looking better.

Don't fall for that. The first reading experience gives you the best reflection of your book's content. Make that first reading experience count during this editing, revising and rewriting phase.

Concluding Step 6**: **Step 6 is all about editing, revising and rewriting. A good novel goes through several rounds of professional editing before it is ready to be published. So spend as much time on editing as possible

CONCLUSION

So this concludes our e-book, "The Step-by-Step Guide to Writing a Novel for Fiction writers and Novelist."

Hopefully, now you have enough knowledge and skills to write your own novel. From brainstorming to selecting ideas; from outlining themes to character development; and from writing your first draft to revising, rewriting and editing, you have learned about every necessary aspect of novel-writing.

The rest depends on you. Just find a solid idea to write about, create interesting characters, and write your heart out. With the lessons learned in this book, you will do just fine. Good luck!

15931650R00041

Printed in Great Britain
by Amazon